Contents

Alternative pronunciation of **i /igh/** ....

Alternative pronunciation of **o /oa/** 6

Alternative pronunciation of **a /ai/** 8

Spelling tricky words **one** and **little** 10

Reading tricky words **water** and **want** 12

Alternative pronunciation of **u /yoo/** and **/oo/ (short)** 14

Alternative pronunciation of **e /ee/** 16

Spelling tricky word **do** and the contraction **don't** 18

The contractions **he's**, **she's**, **I'm** 19

Reading tricky words **who**, **whole**, **where** 20

Alternative pronunciation of **ow /oa/** 22

Alternative pronunciation of **ie /ee/** 24

Alternative pronunciation of **ea /e/** 26

Reading tricky words **any**, **many**, **two** 28

Alternative pronunciation of **er /ur/** 30

Alternative pronunciation of **y /ee/** 32

Alternative pronunciation of **y /igh/** 34

Reading tricky words **school** and **work** 36

Alternative pronunciation of **ou /oa/** and **/oo/ (long)** 38

Alternative pronunciation of **ou /u/** 40

The grapheme **oul** 41

Reading tricky words **thought** and **different** 42

Alternative pronunciation of **a /o/** 44

Alternative pronunciation of **ch /c/** and **/sh/** 46

Reading tricky words **friend** and **through** 48

Alternative pronunciation of **g /j/** 50

Alternative pronunciation of **c /s/** 52

Reading tricky words **once** and **eye** 54

Glossary 55

Alternative pronunciation of i /igh/

▶ The grapheme **i** makes the **/i/** sound in words like **fish**, but it makes the **/igh/** sound in words like **child**. Say both sounds.

fish   child

▶ Read the words below. Think about the correct sound for the grapheme **i** in each word. Draw a ring round the word if the grapheme **i** makes the **/igh/** sound as in **child**.

skin   lift   kind

mind   shrink

wild   find   sniff

blind   silent

▶ Read each question. Write **yes** or **no**.

Do you like kind people? _____

Do spiders have houses? _____

Do you like to find spiders? _____

Is there a day called Friday? _____

Should you hug a wild tiger? _____

Could you stay silent all day? _____

Are some boys called Simon? _____

Would you mind having
a mouse as a pet? _____

Alternative pronunciation of o /oa/

▶ The grapheme **o** makes the **/o/** sound in words like **hot**, but it makes the **/oa/** sound in words like **cold**. Say both sounds.

 hot

 cold

▶ Read the words below. Think about the correct sound for the grapheme **o** in each word. Write the word on the post box if the grapheme **o** makes the **/oa/** sound as in **cold**.

stop   old

both   from

told   most

open   cloth

hello soft

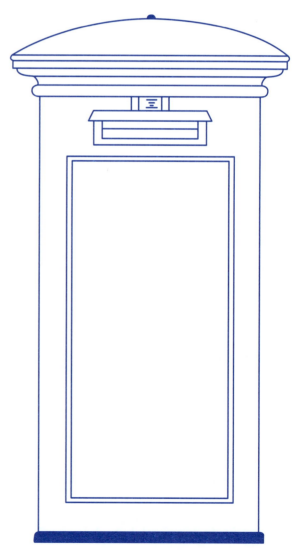

▶ Say the words in sound-talk. All of the words have an **/oa/** sound that is spelt **o**. Write the letters needed to complete each word.

I called to say
___ ___ ___.

Meet Tog. He is our
___ ___ ___ ___.

The cow jumped
___ ___ ___ the moon.

Has your house been
___ ___ ___?

Keep your painting in a
___ ___ ___ ___ ___.

Would you like a pot of
___ ___ ___ ___?

Alternative pronunciation of a /ai/

▶ The grapheme **a** makes the **/a/** sound in words like **map**, but it makes the **/ai/** sound in words like **paper**. Say both sounds.

 map    paper

▶ Use sound-talk to read these words. Draw a line under the word if the grapheme **a** makes the **/ai/** sound as in **paper**. Join each word to the correct picture.

dragon

wafer

apron

balloon

paperclip

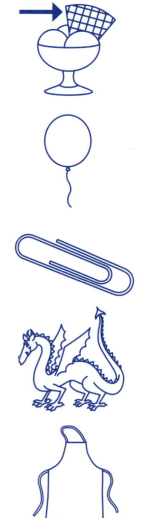

▶ Read each sentence and the two words below it. Choose the word that makes sense in the sentence and write it on the line.

Meet me here _____.

later   layer

I asked for eggs and _____.

bacon   banjo

A cook would use a _____.

hamster   grater

The oak tree grew from an _____.

apron   acorn

The new boy was called _____.

David   Friday

Mr Day looked in his _____.

sandpaper   newspaper

Spelling tricky words **one** and **little**

▶ Read the tricky word. Then copy the word.

one _____ _____ _____

▶ Look at the pictures. Write the missing number as a word to complete each sentence.

 Our house is number _____.

 Here are _____ gold coins.

 I have _____ pet mouse.

 Mr Old took _____ photo.

 We found _____ acorns.

▶ Read the tricky word. Look at the tricky part. Then copy the word.

li**tt**le _____ _____ _____

▶ Look at the pictures. Write the tricky words **one**, **little** and the other missing word to complete each caption.

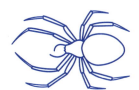 ___one___   ___little___   ___spider___

 _____ _____ _____

 _____ _____ _____

 _____ _____ _____

 _____ _____ _____

Phonics Practice Pupil Book 6

Reading tricky words **water** and **want**

▶ Read the tricky word. Look out for the tricky part.

water
• • —

▶ Read each question. Write **yes** or **no**.

Could water turn into gold? _____

Should people drink water? _____

Would a stone float on water? _____

Should we water our garden? _____

Would you swim in cold water? _____

Would a paper bag hold water? _____

Would a hippo swim in water? _____

▶ Read the tricky word. Look out for the tricky part.

w**a**nt
• • • •

▶ Read the sentences. Join each sentence to the correct picture.

I want a new house.

We want a robot to make our tea.

I want you to find me a pot of gold.

Water! I want some water.

I want to grind this corn.

Phonics Practice Pupil Book 6

Alternative pronunciation of u /yoo/ and /oo/ (short)

▶ The grapheme **u** makes the **/u/** sound in words like **sun**, but it makes the **/yoo/** sound in words like **unicorn**. It can also make the short **/oo/** sound in words like **pull** for some people. Say the three sounds.

s**u**n   **u**nicorn   p**u**ll

▶ Read the words below. Think about the correct sound for the grapheme **u** in each word. Draw a ring round the word if the grapheme **u** makes the **/yoo/** sound as in **unicorn**.

awful   pushing   stupid

pudding   human   music

units   bull   tulip   bush

▶ Read each question. Draw a ring round the three correct answers.

Which of these could people read?

a menu   a newspaper   a bush   a poster

Which of these are flowers?

paperclips   tulips   buttercups   bluebells

Which do people play music on?

a tuba   tuna   a banjo   a trumpet

Which of these have no horns?

uniforms   unicorns   humans   umbrellas

Which of these might people want to eat?

a pudding   butter   a mango   units

Alternative pronunciation of e /ee/

▶ The grapheme **e** makes the /e/ sound in words like **egg**, but it makes the /ee/ sound in words like **me**. Say both sounds.

egg   me

▶ Read the words below. Think about the correct sound for the grapheme **e** in each word. Draw a ring round the word if the grapheme **e** makes the /ee/ sound as in **me**.

tenth   she's   we

spend   maybe

evil   email   enter

secret   selfish

▶ Read each sentence and the two words below it. Choose the word that makes sense in the sentence and write it on the line.

Leroy told me a _____.

secret   second

She stood right _____ me.

bedtime   behind

He tried to _____ her name.

remember   remain

Peter wants to send an _____.

email   elephant.

We want you to run in the _____.

relay   delay

Mr Roy pulled the _____ down.

fever   lever

Spelling tricky word **do** and the contraction **don't**

▶ Read the tricky word **do** and the contraction **don't**. The contraction **don't** is a shortened form of **do not**. Look at the tricky part in the first word. Then copy the words.

do _____   don't _____

▶ Read each question. Write **I do** or **I don't**.

Do you like being cold?   _____ .

Do you have a robot?   _____ .

Do you ever tell secrets?   _____ .

Do you ever eat paper?   _____ .

Do you do as you are told?   _____ .

Do you want some pudding?   _____ .

Do you have a blue uniform?   _____ .

The contractions he's, she's, I'm

The words below are also contractions (shortened forms). The apostrophe goes in the place of the missing letter.

he's   she's   I'm

▶ Write the correct shortened form to complete each sentence.

Omar says _____ feeling cold.

Kate thinks _____ come first.

Eve says _____ late again.

_____ quick so he comes first.

He tries to get out but _____ stuck.

I don't think _____ going to make it to the game.

Reading tricky words **who**, **whole**, **where**

▶ Read the tricky words. Look out for the tricky parts.

who   **whole**

▶ Read the sentences. Join each sentence to the correct picture.

Who ate a whole tube of sweets?

Who drank the whole lake?

Who painted the whole town blue?

Who found a whole pack full of seeds?

Who ate the fish whole?

▶ Read the tricky word. Look out for the tricky part.

wh*ere*

▶ Read each question. Draw a ring round the correct answer.

Where could you find a tiger?

in the post   in the wild   in a case

Who would have a gold crown?

a queen   an old man   a child

Where would you find tulips?

in zoos   in gardens   in the sea

Who could have a uniform?

a hippo   a child   a robot

Alternative pronunciation of ow /oa/

▶ The grapheme **ow** makes the **/ow/** sound in words like **cow**, but it makes the **/oa/** sound in words like **snow**. Say both sounds.

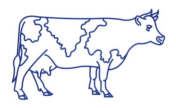 cow

 snow

▶ Read the words below. Think about the correct sound for the grapheme **ow** in each word. Draw a ring round the word if the grapheme **ow** makes the **/oa/** sound as in **snow**.

show   tower   slow

blow   powder

throw   down   crowd

low   shadow

▶ Say the words in sound-talk. All of the words have an **/oa/** sound that is spelt **ow**. Write the letters needed to complete each word.

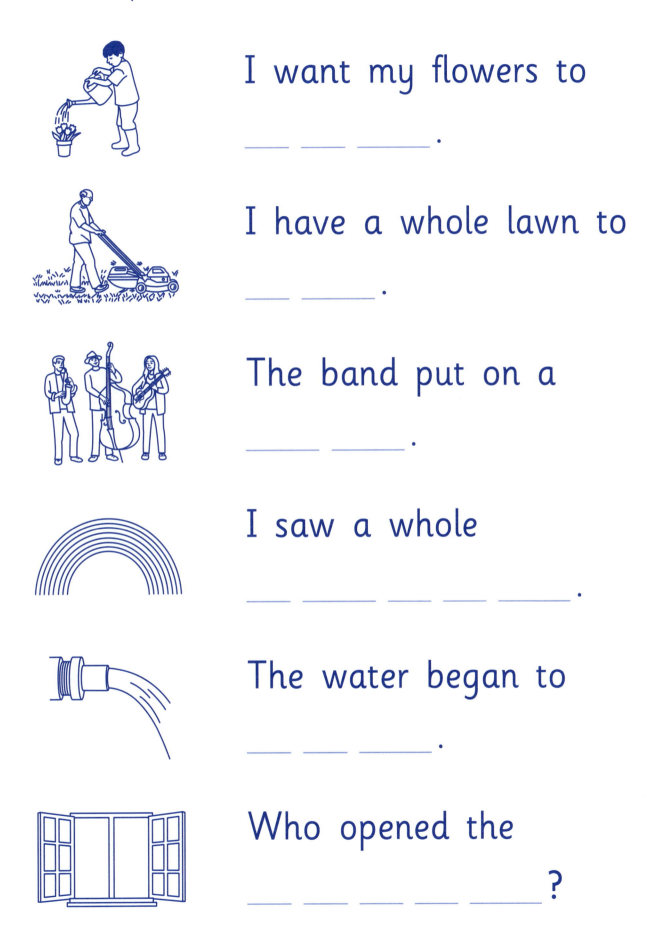

I want my flowers to __ __ ___ .

I have a whole lawn to __ __ .

The band put on a ___ ___ .

I saw a whole __ __ __ __ ___ .

The water began to __ __ __ .

Who opened the __ __ __ __ ___ ?

Alternative pronunciation of ie /ee/

▶ The grapheme **ie** makes the **/igh/** sound in words like **tie**, but it makes the **/ee/** sound in words like **field**. Say both sounds.

 tie    field

▶ Use sound-talk to read these words. Draw a line under the word if the grapheme **ie** makes the **/ee/** sound as in **field**. Join each word to the correct picture.

thief

shield

cookie

bow tie

briefcase

▶ Read each question. Draw a ring round the correct answer.

Who might be sent to jail?

| a thief | a robot | a snake |

Where do cows graze?

| in a file | in a pie | in a field |

Who flies a plane?

| a hippo | a pilot | a priest |

What is a loud sound?

| a shield | a shadow | a shriek |

What is a sort of photo?

| a selfie | a smoothie | a cookie |

Phonics Practice Pupil Book 6

Alternative pronunciation of ea /e/

▶ The grapheme **ea** makes the **/ee/** sound in words like **eat**, but it makes the **/e/** sound in words like **bread**. Say both sounds.

 eat  bread

▶ Read the words below. Think about the correct sound for the grapheme **ea** in each word. Write the word on the slice of bread if the grapheme **ea** makes the **/e/** sound as in **bread**.

steal   deaf

clean   spread

feather   weather

dead   feast

threat   scream

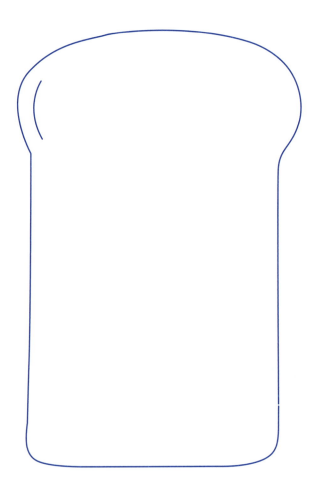

▶ Read each sentence and the three words below it. Choose the word that makes sense in the sentence and write it on the line.

I _____ the whole book.

dead   read   reach

He was puffing and out of _____.

thread   dread   breath

The spilt water began to _____.

spread   scream   said

Who can stand on their _____?

health   heap   head

In the heat, he began to _____.

seal   steal   sweat

I want peanut butter on my _____.

bead   bread   bed

Reading tricky words **any**, **many**, **two**

▶ Read the tricky words. Look out for the tricky parts.

▶ Look at each picture and read the question. Write the correct answer.

 How many spiders? _____

 Are there any sheep? _____

 How many beads? _____

 How many bowls? _____

 Are there any pillows? _____

▶ Read the tricky word. Look out for the tricky part.

two

▶ Read the captions. Finish the picture to go with each caption.

two buttons on the snowman

two bows in her hair

two lines down the shield

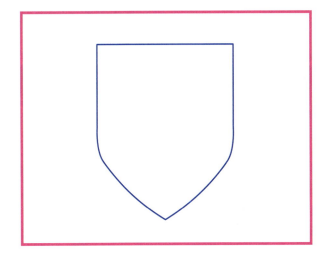

two fried eggs for breakfast

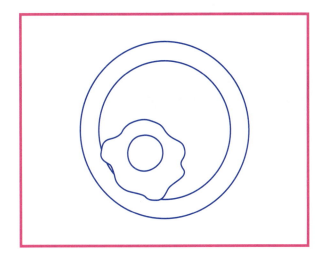

Alternative pronunciation of er /ur/

▶ The grapheme **er** makes the **/er/** sound in words like **ladder**, but it makes the **/ur/** sound in words like **fern**. Say both sounds.

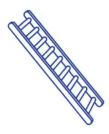 ladder

 fern

▶ Use sound-talk to read these words. Draw a line under the grapheme **er** that makes the **/ur/** sound as in **fern**. Join each word to the correct picture.

herbs

perch

person

perfume

kerb

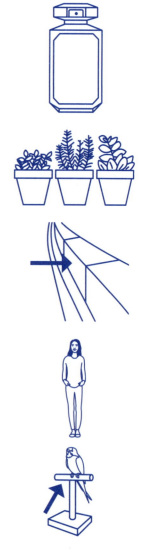

▶ Read each question. Write **yes** or **no**.

Are some people stern? _____

Have you met any mermaids? _____

Are there two terms in a year? _____

Are there many sorts of herbs? _____

Do birds perch on clouds? _____

Are there many cows in a herd? _____

Have you ever met a person called Fern? _____

Have you ever met a dog expert? _____

Alternative pronunciation of y /ee/

▶ The grapheme **y** makes the **/y/** sound in words like **yoyo**, but it makes the **/ee/** sound at the end of words like **happy**. Say both sounds.

 yoyo    happy

▶ Use sound-talk to read the two words on each line. Draw a line under the grapheme **y** if it makes the **/ee/** sound as in **happy**. Tick the word that goes with the picture.

🍮	jolly ☐	jelly ☐
🍦	lorry ☐	lolly ☐
👶	baby ☐	body ☐
15	fifteen ☐	fifty ☐
🍬	yellow ☐	yummy ☐

▶ Read each clue and the answers below it. Draw a ring round all the correct answers.

Water that is not clean is …

| dreary | dizzy | dirty |

Someone who needs food is …

| happy | hungry | hairy |

These are two sorts of flower.

| daisy | penny | poppy |

These are two parts of your body.

| teddy | tummy | elbow |

These are two things found underwater.

| dolphin | party | jellyfish |

Alternative pronunciation of y /igh/

▶ The grapheme **y** makes the /y/ sound in words like **yoyo** and the /ee/ sound at the end of words like **happy**. The grapheme **y** can also make the /igh/ sound at the end of words like **fly**. Say the three sounds.

yoyo   happy   fly

▶ Read the words below. Think about the correct sound for the grapheme **y** in each word. Write each word in the correct box to show the sound made by the grapheme **y**.

year   cry   yellow   yelp   spy
funny   very   dry   easy

▶ Write the missing word **fly**, **by**, **cry** or **why** to complete each sentence. Join each sentence to the correct picture.

A baby began to _____ .

Most birds can _____ .

Two boats float _____ .

_____ do people fry fish?

Two kites _____ in the sky.

The sly fox hid _____ the water.

Reading tricky words **school** and **work**

▶ Read the tricky word. Look out for the tricky part.

school

▶ Read each question. Draw a ring round all the correct answers.

What might you find in a school?

a pigsty	an alphabet	a globe
a jelly	a shield	a crayon
a phonics book	a drawing	a storybook

What might you try doing in school?

counting	flying	spreading
reading	drawing	spying
throwing	frying	growing

36   Schofield & Sims · My Letters and Sounds

▶ Read the tricky word. Look out for the tricky part.

w**or**k

▶ Read each question. Write **yes** or **no**.

Do teachers work in schools? _____

Could a baby work in a shop? _____

Do phones work underwater? _____

Do you work hard at school? _____

Do farmers work in fields? _____

Do you have any homework? _____

Will a lorry work without any wheels? _____

Alternative pronunciation of ou /oa/ and /oo/ (long)

▶ The grapheme **ou** makes the **/ow/** sound in words like **cloud**, but it makes the **/oa/** sound in words like **shoulder**. Say both sounds.

 cloud    shoulder

▶ Use sound-talk to read these words. Draw a line under the word if the grapheme **ou** makes the **/oa/** sound as in **shoulder**. Join each word to the correct picture.

mould

mountain

boulder

smoulder

spout

▶ The grapheme **ou** can also make the long **/oo/** sound in words like **soup**. Say the sound.

 soup

▶ Read the sentences. Draw a line under any word where the grapheme **ou** makes the long **/oo/** sound as in **soup**.

I like to work in a group.

Do you have two shoulders?

I don't want any mouldy soup.

Count how many coupons I have.

Are you proud of your schoolwork?

Grandad worked hard in his youth.

I found a toucan sitting on a big round boulder.

Phonics Practice Pupil Book 6

Alternative pronunciation of ou /u/

▶ The grapheme **ou** makes the **/ow/** sound in words like **cloud**, the **/oa/** sound in words like **shoulder**, and the long **/oo/** sound in words like **soup**. The grapheme **ou** can also make the **/u/** sound in words like **country**. Say the sound.

 country

▶ Read the words below. Think about the correct sound for the grapheme **ou** in each word. Draw a ring round the word if the grapheme **ou** makes the **/u/** sound as in **country**.

touch   boulder

mould   you   group

cousin   loud   young

pound   amount

The grapheme oul

The /u/ or short /oo/ sound is spelt **oul** in the words **could**, **would** and **should**.

could

▶ Read each sentence. Tick the sentence if it is true.

I could touch the clouds. ☐

I could carry a heavy boulder. ☐

I shouldn't eat mouldy bread. ☐

I would work well in a group. ☐

I couldn't count up to thirty. ☐

I shouldn't touch a hot campfire. ☐

I would like to try beetroot soup. ☐

I would like to visit a new country. ☐

Reading tricky words **thought** and **different**

▶ Read the tricky word. Look out for the tricky part.

thought

▶ Read the sentences. Join each sentence to the correct picture.

The little mouse thought he could help.

An old lady thought she would make soup.

The sly fox thought of a clever plan.

A young boy thought he could touch the sky.

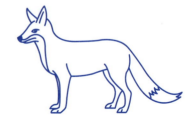

▶ Read the tricky word. Look out for the tricky part.

diff**er**ent

▶ Read the instructions. Draw a picture to go with each instruction.

Make one line a different size.	Draw two different shapes.
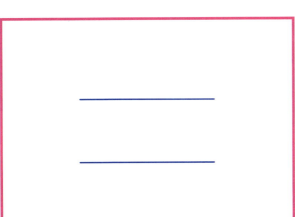	

Make the bowls look different.	Draw a different sort of cake.
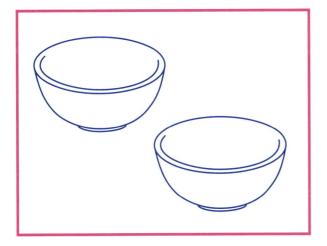	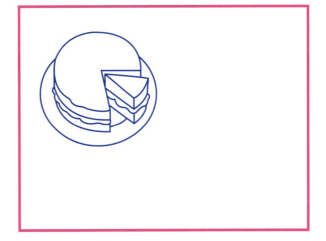

Alternative pronunciation of a /o/

▶ The grapheme **a** makes the **/a/** sound in words like **map**, the **/ai/** sound in words like **paper** and the **/o/** sound in words like **wash**. Say the three sounds.

m**a**p   p**a**per   w**a**sh

▶ Read the words below. Think about the correct sound for the grapheme **a** in each word. Draw a ring round the word if the grapheme **a** makes the **/o/** sound as in **wash**.

was   wasp   snap

wand   washing

swan   stand   swap

scrap   squash

▶ Read the questions and the possible answers. Write the missing word or words **what**, **want** or **wash** to complete each question. Draw a ring round the correct answer.

__What__ are bowls made from?

| soap | (china) | jelly |

_____ will an acorn grow into?

| a swan | a human | an oak tree |

_____ can fly in the sky?

| a wallet | a wasp | a daisy |

_____ might you _____ for dinner?

| stone | swap | soup |

_____ do you _____ in water?

| bread | boulders | hands |

Phonics Practice Pupil Book 6

Alternative pronunciation of ch /c/ and /sh/

▶ The grapheme **ch** makes the **/ch/** sound in words like **chick**, but it makes the **/c/** sound in words like **school**. Say both sounds.

 chick

 school

▶ Read the words below. Think about the correct sound for the grapheme **ch** in each word. Draw a ring round the word if the grapheme **ch** makes the **/c/** sound as in **school**.

chief   ache   chorus

children   Chrissy

cheat   echo   chemist

chewing   orchestra

▶ The grapheme **ch** can also make the **/sh/** sound in words like **chef**. Say the sound.

 chef

▶ Read the sentences. Draw a line under any word where the grapheme **ch** makes the **/sh/** sound as in **chef**. Join each sentence to the correct picture.

The parachute is open.

Chris works as a chef.

Archie tried the water chute.

A chemist sells many different pills.

Charlene sang the whole chorus.

Reading tricky words **friend** and **through**

▶ Read the tricky word. Look out for the tricky part.

friend
•• — •• •

▶ Read the two sentences and look at the picture. Tick the sentence that goes with the picture.

Ellie had a friend called Sophie. ☐

Ellie had a friend called Harry. ☐

Annie the ant met her friend Billy the butterfly. ☐

Ant went to find her friend Wendy the wasp. ☐

▶ Read the tricky word. Look out for the tricky part.

through

▶ Read each sentence and the two words below it. Choose the word that makes sense in the sentence and write it on the line.

Don't try to go through a _____.

swamp   swan

Follow the trail through the _____.

wand   wood

He couldn't get through the _____.

hole   howl

A plane flew through the _____.

sky   sly

She looked through the _____.

washing   window

Alternative pronunciation of g /j/

▶ The grapheme **g** makes the **/g/** sound in words like **goat**, but it makes the **/j/** sound before **e**, **i** and **y** in words like **gem**. Say both sounds.

 goat

 gem

▶ Read the words below. Think about the correct sound for the grapheme **g** in each word. Draw a ring round the word if the grapheme **g** makes the **/j/** sound as in **gem**.

golf   gulped   giant

magic   germ

game   target   ginger

huge   danger

▶ Read each question. Write **yes** or **no**.

Is a giant huge? _____

Are tigers endangered? _____

Do you use shower gel? _____

Do you own a magic wand? _____

Have you ever been on stage? _____

Could you be a secret agent? _____

Are there different sorts of germs? _____

Do you have a friend with ginger hair? _____

Alternative pronunciation of c /s/

▶ The grapheme **c** makes the **/c/** sound in words like **cat**, but it makes the **/s/** sound before **e**, **i** and **y** in words like **city**. Say both sounds.

 cat    city

▶ Use sound-talk to read these words. Draw a line under the word if the grapheme **c** makes the **/s/** sound as in **city**. Join each word to the correct picture.

comic

ice cube

cactus

saucer

princess

▶ Read each clue and the answers below it. Draw a ring round the correct answer.

This is where you see stars.

| in spice | in space | in ice |

This is where you see clowns.

| in a cell | at a circus | at a counter |

This is what you call a bit of cake.

| a slice | a place | a roll |

This is where my friend keeps mice.

| in a case | on stage | in a cage |

This is a sort of party.

| candy | fancy dress | daisy chain |

Reading tricky words **once** and **eye**

▶ Read the tricky words.

once   eye

▶ Read the sentences. Join each sentence to the correct picture.

The ginger cat opened one eye.

Once there was a funny clown.

Once there was a giant with just one eye.

The gingerbread man had two little eyes.

There was once a princess with eyes like gemstones.